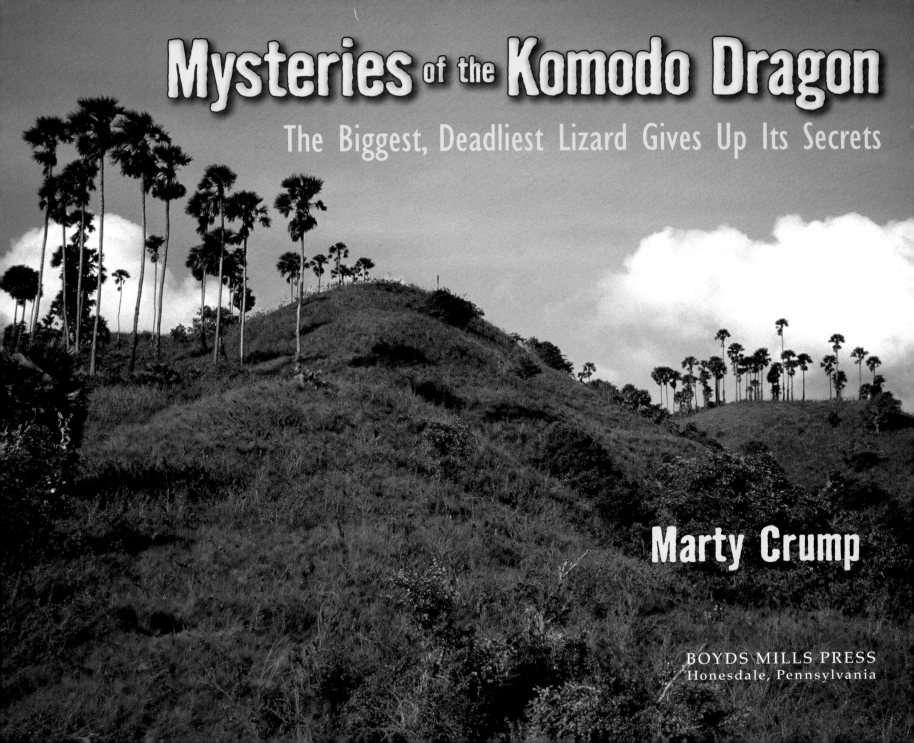

# Mysteries of the Komodo Dragon

## The Biggest, Deadliest Lizard Gives Up Its Secrets

## Marty Crump

BOYDS MILLS PRESS
Honesdale, Pennsylvania

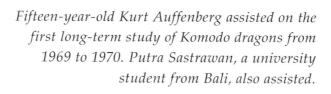

Komodo dragons, the world's largest lizards, can weigh more than 200 pounds (91 kilograms) and measure up to 10 feet (3 meters). Local islanders call their giant lizards ora, meaning "grandfather" or "grandmother," or buaja darat, meaning "land crocodile."

Fifteen-year-old Kurt Auffenberg assisted on the first long-term study of Komodo dragons from 1969 to 1970. Putra Sastrawan, a university student from Bali, also assisted.

# A SEVEN-FOOT BEAST—

a living dragon—crept through the tall grass toward a campsite, flicking his forked, yellow tongue. Fifteen-year-old Kurt and his companion, Putra, nervously watched from nearby as the dragon entered their tent. Inside, the dragon raided a backpack. He shredded a shirt with his long claws and sharp teeth. Then he darted into the forest carrying a used handkerchief.

Kurt and Putra packed up and hiked 2½ miles (4 kilometers) back home. The next day, the same Komodo dragon laid his chin on the open deck of Kurt's house and watched the people inside. Later, Kurt and Putra inspected the trail. The dragon's tracks followed their footprints. Had the dragon been stalking them for dinner?

To answer dragon mysteries, many people have traveled to the Indonesian Lesser Sunda Islands where these dragons live. Some have been students like Kurt and Putra. Others have been scientists or people who collect animals for museums and zoos. Few people live on these remote islands. The land is rugged, temperatures are hot, and fresh water is scarce. Neighboring volcanoes spew smoke and ash. Strong waves lash the shores. The ocean boils and churns as if to warn, "GO AWAY!"

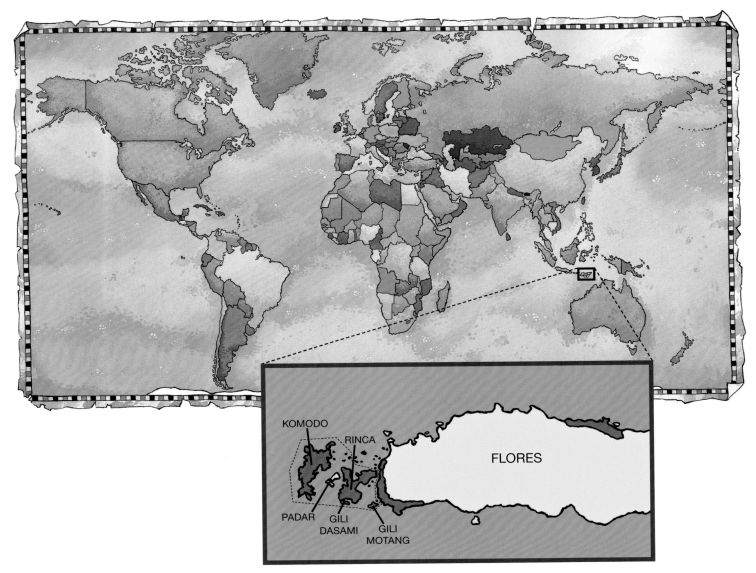

*Komodo dragons live only on five Lesser Sunda Islands of Indonesia, in the areas colored green. The lizards are most common on Komodo Island. Four of the islands are included in Komodo National Park, whose boundaries are indicated by the dotted lines. Komodo dragons disappeared from Padar in the late 1970s, likely because poachers and wild dogs killed many of their main prey—deer.*

Thousands of years ago, Chinese sailors probably visited the Lesser Sunda Islands to collect Komodo dragon skins. Their tales of giant lizards may have formed the basis for imaginary dragons. Later, ancient maps of the area warned travelers "Here there be dragons."

Rumors of giant reptiles probably kept most people away from these islands. The first people to live on Komodo Island were criminals, who were banished there over a century ago. They learned that the dragons were real!

In 1910, a Dutch soldier named van Hensbroek heard about the gigantic reptiles. He wondered: Do they really exist? If so, what are they?

Van Hensbroek sailed to Komodo. He shot a dragon and sent the skin and a photograph to the museum director in Java, one of the main islands in Indonesia. The museum director wondered: What could this be? He hired a collector to bring him some specimens. After seeing the whole animal, the director recognized it as a monitor lizard and gave it the scientific name *Varanus komodoensis*—the monitor from Komodo.

For more than the next decade, rumors circulated that the creatures grew to 20 feet (6 meters)—half the length of *Tyrannosaurus rex*.

*Komodo dragons flick their yellow, forked tongues in and out of their mouths to smell the air and ground—as snakes do. Their tongues pick up scent particles and guide the dragons to food.*

*Like Komodo dragons, mythical Asian dragons are scaly beasts with long claws, sharp teeth, and powerful tails.*

*Komodo dragons walk along the beaches and eat dead animals such as fish and turtles.*
*Their teeth are jagged like a steak knife—great for cutting flesh. The longest teeth are about 3/4 inch (2 centimeters) long.*

In 1926, W. Douglas Burden, naturalist and adventurer, led the first "dragon hunt" to Komodo from the United States. He wanted to learn about the lizards' eating habits.

Burden's assistants built screens, or blinds, from branches. They put a dead deer or wild boar as bait on one side of the blind. Burden waited on the other side.

Tongue-flicking monitors lumbered up to the smelly bait. Sharp claws and teeth tore at the carcass. The dragons hissed at one another. They gulped huge chunks of meat and bone. One dragon swallowed the hindquarters of a wild boar all at once—skin, hoofs, legs, bones, and all. But they didn't eat Burden.

To catch dragons, the team made spring traps. Burden's assistants bent trees and fastened the tops to the ground. The men set a dead animal and a noose at the front of each trap. When a lizard stuck its head through the noose to reach the bait, the tree flew back up. The men then lassoed the thrashing, angry lizard. Burden concluded that the largest dragons were 10 feet (3 meters) long—one quarter the size of *Tyrannosaurus rex*.

*Komodo dragons sometimes swim in the ocean.*

Burden left with a dozen skins and two live dragons. The live dragons soon died, but several skins were stuffed and mounted for the American Museum of Natural History. Some still stand in the museum. In magazine articles about his adventure, Burden called Komodo monitors "dragon lizards." The name *dragon* stuck.

Later expeditions caught dragons for zoos. From these captives, we learned about dragon personalities. Some are aggressive, some are shy, and others are easygoing. Bübchen (the German word for "sweetie pie") was a favorite in Germany. Like a gentle puppy, she walked on a leash through the zoo grounds. Sumbawa, housed at the London Zoo, daintily ate chicken eggs from a tablespoon. Bübchen and Sumbawa showed the world another side of Komodo dragons. Well-fed captives could be gentle giants.

*Viewing Komodo dragons in zoos allows the public to appreciate these exotic reptiles. By understanding the daily requirements of Komodo dragons, we can help protect the species.*

*Young dragons live in trees for the first two years. That way they avoid cannibalistic adults, which are too big to climb trees. The young dragons forage for insects and small lizards on the bark.*

By the late 1960s, Komodo dragons were disappearing. Only about 1,100 were thought to be alive.

Would they become extinct? Dr. F. Wayne King, from the Bronx Zoo, suggested that, to save the dragons, we needed to learn more about them.

Dr. Walter Auffenberg, a herpetologist at the University of Florida, offered to conduct the study—if his family agreed. After discussion at the dinner table, his wife, Elinor, and their three sons, ages five, eight, and fifteen (Kurt), voted an enthusiastic yes!

*The Auffenberg family lived here on Komodo Island for eleven months.*
*They ate lots of rice, fish, coconuts, and bananas, and they sampled the local squid, oysters, and crabs.*

Kurt hiked along the island's coast, through mangrove forests, savannas, bamboo forests, and up and over the mountains looking for dragons. It was during one of these trips that Kurt and Putra encountered the handkerchief-loving dragon. Kurt tracked dragons through tunnels that the dragons bulldozed in dense grass. His heart pounded as he crept around each turn, wondering if he'd come eyeball to eyeball with a hungry dragon as big as a grizzly bear.

*To watch and track individuals, Walter Auffenberg needed to tell the lizards apart.*
*He attached numbered tags, and he spray-painted numbers on the lizards' sides.*

Walter Auffenberg wanted to learn everything possible about the dragons. He marked individuals and watched them from various places—a platform perched in a tree, a tower, and blinds on the ground.

Wild dragons have different personalities, just as captives do. Most ran from Auffenberg, but some stood their ground and hissed or threatened with open mouths. Some even entered the blinds and drove Auffenberg out. Komodo dragons occasionally bite, kill, and eat people.

To discover how much area the dragons need, Auffenberg tracked the dragons' footprints in the volcanic ash and measured distances traveled. He also attached radio transmitters to lizards and recorded their movements. Some adults traveled 6 miles (10 kilometers) in one day. These monitors need a lot of space.

Walter Auffenberg (wearing hat), Kurt Auffenberg (in foreground with back to camera), and Putra Sastrawan (left), caught dragons in traps. They weighed, measured, and marked each one.

Walter Auffenberg sat behind a blind and peered out a peephole to watch Komodo dragons interact as they ate the bait.

*A full-grown Komodo dragon can kill a 1,300-pound (590-kilogram) water buffalo.*

Burden had described *how* Komodo dragons eat. Auffenberg wanted to find out *what* they eat. To learn more about meat-eating animals, biologists often study their droppings to identify bones, fur, feathers, and other body parts of the prey the animals have eaten but did not completely digest. After analyzing 4,267 droppings, Auffenberg found that dragons eat mostly deer, wild boar, black rats—and other Komodo dragons.

Komodo dragons eat dead animals, but they also kill living prey. Auffenberg wondered how these reptiles kill fast-running mammals that are even larger than themselves. He found they sometimes attack sleeping animals. They also ambush prey. Often they grab their victims' legs or throats and throw them to the ground. Sometimes the prey bleed to death where they fall, but often they escape. Auffenberg wondered: What happens to these animals?

*Deer are the most common prey eaten by adult Komodo dragons.*

*Komodo dragons can gulp down over 5 pounds (2.3 kilograms) of food per minute—faster than any predator known, except for large snakes. Walter Auffenberg watched a 110-pound (50-kilogram) female dragon eat an entire wild boar weighing 68 pounds (31 kilograms) in seventeen minutes.*

Within a few days, most wounded prey die from a single dragon's bite. Why? Auffenberg suspected that because these lizards feast on rotting flesh full of bacteria, their own saliva might contain deadly bacteria. If so, when a Komodo dragon bites into prey, the bacteria might cause infection.

Auffenberg collected saliva from two

*A Komodo dragon can eat more than half its body weight in a single meal.*
*A large adult typically eats one large prey per month.*

dragons. Other scientists later identified four different kinds of deadly bacteria from the saliva.

Mystery solved. A dragon bites its prey. Saliva bacteria infect the wound and later kill the prey. Since Komodo dragons can sniff out dead animals from 7 miles (11 kilometers) away, monitors descend on the rotting carcass and feast. Deadly dragon drool is the "secret" killing weapon.

But there's another mystery. . . .

In the early 1990s, Terry Fredeking, president of a biotechnology company, asked, "What can we do next that's dangerous, exciting, and will advance science?"

His consultant suggested Komodo dragons. The man described the giant lizards and their deadly drool. Then he described the teeth—a dentist's nightmare.

Spongy gums cover two-thirds of each jagged-edged tooth. When a dragon bites, the gums slide toward the bone, exposing even more of each tooth. As the sharp tooth edges rub over the gums, they break the skin. Deadly bacteria enter these damaged gums. The lizards also trade bacteria when they bite each other while fighting over food.

The consultant asked, Why don't the lizards get infected from their own deadly bacteria?

Fredeking's response: "That's it. Lead me to 'em!"

Fredeking thought the dragons might have undiscovered substances that protect them from their bacteria. If so, could these substances be isolated and made into drugs to fight infections in humans?

*Male Komodo dragons wrestle for females. The largest and strongest males usually win.*

*Imagine a dozen drooling, tongue-flicking dragons heading toward you!*

In 1995, Fredeking collected saliva from dragons on Komodo Island. He and his crew hid in the bushes. When a dragon wandered by, the crew slipped a noose over its head. Several men held down the lizard. Others wrapped duct tape around the snout and claws. One person collected saliva with a long cotton swab. Another person drew a blood sample from a vein in the tail.

One day, after the team had captured a big lizard, more than a dozen drooling dragons headed toward them. The dragons had been attracted by the noisy struggle and intended to

*Komodo dragons rule this volcanic island, Komodo. The island is small—about 22 miles (35.4 kilometers) long and 12 miles (19.3 kilometers) wide. Much of the year, the weather is dry and hot. Temperatures sometimes rise above 120 degrees Fahrenheit (49 degrees Celsius). To escape the scorching heat, dragons rest in burrows.*

eat their comrade—and perhaps the men as well. The men used sticks to prod the lizards that now surrounded them. Finally, the lizards lumbered away.

Fredeking sighed, "Man, oh man, what we do for science."

Fredeking's samples of dragon spit and blood held surprises. Researchers found fifty-four potentially deadly kinds of bacteria from the saliva. Plus, three substances in the dragon blood might work as new antibiotics—drugs to help us fight bacterial infections.

*Komodo dragons dig holes into which they lay their eggs.
Just as mythical dragons guard treasure, some mother dragons guard their nests.*

*Sometimes the nest chamber is more than 5 feet (1.5 meters) deep.*

Komodo dragons have another surprising trick up their scales.

In 2006, a dragon in the London Zoo laid eggs. She hadn't been with a male for over two years, yet four eggs hatched. All were males. How had the eggs become fertilized? A year later, a dragon in another zoo laid twenty-five eggs. She had never been kept with a male, yet seven eggs hatched. Again, all the baby dragons were males. Had these two females escaped in the night and found males to mate with?

Tests revealed a surprise. The eggs had not been fertilized by males. The hatchlings were dragons without dads.

Usually, a fertilized egg gets one set of chromosomes from each parent. Chromosomes

*Komodo dragons typically lay eighteen to thirty eggs per clutch. The tough, leathery eggs are about 3 inches (7.6 centimeters) long. They hatch in about eight months. Babies are about 15 to 18 inches (38 to 46 centimeters) long when they hatch.*

are threadlike structures that carry genetic material. But these females had reproduced by *parthenogenesis*: the mothers' chromosomes had doubled to form the full set. Because of the way sex is determined in these lizards, parthenogenetic dragons are always males.

What does this mean for Komodo dragons?

Imagine a female getting washed onto a dragon-less island during a storm. Even though she finds no males, she can lay eggs that will hatch. This one female could establish a new colony. She will produce all males, but later she can mate with her sons and produce both sons and daughters.

23

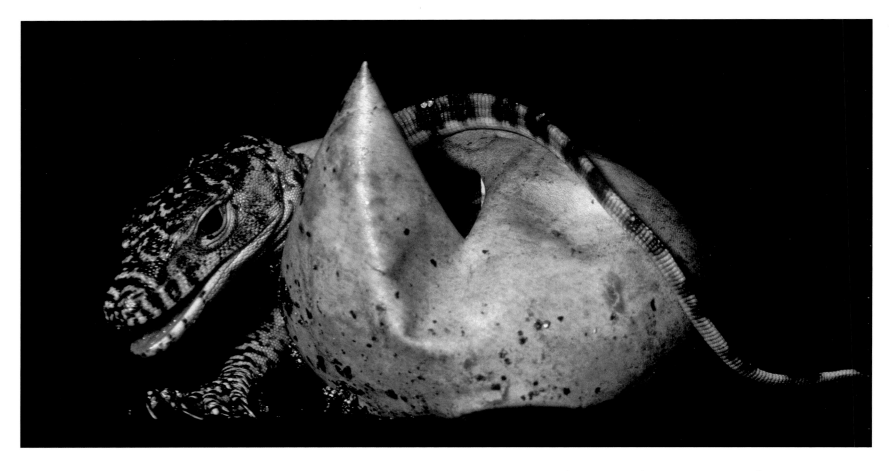

*Kraken, named after the legendary sea monsters that supposedly lived off the coast of Norway, was the first Komodo dragon born in captivity outside of Indonesia. She hatched in 1992.*

Puppies, kittens, and monkeys love to play. But dragons? A young Komodo dragon that lived in the National Zoo in Washington, D.C., made dragon history.

When President Reagan visited the Indonesian island of Bali in 1986, Indonesia's leader, President Soeharto, gave a pair of Komodo dragons to the people of the United States.

Six years later, the female laid twenty-six eggs. A female dragon named Kraken was the first to hatch.

Most reptiles ignore any objects that are not food. But when Kraken was three years old, she started to play with objects. She stuck her head into a plastic bucket and trotted around. She nudged Frisbees and rubber rings with her snout and carried those around as well.

Kraken pulled a handkerchief out of her keeper's back pocket. When he reached down to grab it, she pulled back. The two played tug-of-war—like a kid and a dog. They also played tug-of-war with plastic cups and soda cans.

*Despite our obvious differences, Indonesian legends tell of the oneness of humans and Komodo dragons. Some villagers believe the dragons are their brothers and sisters.*

*Smaug's ball is filled with ten dead rats. He rolls the ball with his snout or foot until part of a rat sticks out from a hole. After he eats the rat, he rolls the ball again. It takes him about five minutes to eat all ten rats.*

Besides allowing us to see exotic animals and learn about their behavior, zoos keep rare species alive. What if all wild Komodo dragons died because of a massive volcanic eruption? At least we would still have dragons in zoos, and perhaps their offspring could be released into the wild. Now we know how to care for Komodo dragons—so they stay healthy and breed.

One favorite dragon is Smaug, cared for by Judith Bryja at the Houston Zoo. Smaug has

*Smaug has never been aggressive toward his caretaker, Judith Bryja. Fortunately for keepers, the saliva bacteria of captive dragons are not as deadly as those of wild dragons, since captives don't eat rotting meat.*

good days and bad days. On his good days, he lets Judith trim his nails and wash his face. On his "bratty" days, he knocks over his water dish.

Smaug usually sits at the front of the exhibit as if to say, "Admire me." Judith says, "People often think that he eyes young children hungrily." She knows, of course, that he doesn't. He's one of the gentle giants.

Komodo National Park, established in 1980, protects the dragons on four islands of Indonesia. Every year, thousands of tourists visit the park. Two reserves protect the monitors on Flores Island.

Komodo dragons survive their harsh environment in many ways. They rest in burrows to escape the heat. They can kill their prey with one bite. Females can reproduce without mates.

Still, their survival depends on us. People are the only predators of adult dragons. For this reason, they have been protected most of the time since they were "discovered" by scientists. Without a permit, it is illegal to catch or kill a Komodo dragon.

Field biologists continue to unravel dragon mysteries. Achmad Ariefiandy, from Java, is a student at Melbourne University in Australia and a researcher with the Komodo Survival Program. He is studying what wild dragons need to stay healthy and to reproduce. Scientists build on the research of others. Achmad has received valuable advice from Putra Sastrawan—who was once a student from Bali and helped Walter Auffenberg study the dragons so many years ago.

*Biologist Achmad Ariefiandy (center) and two assistants from Komodo Island use huge live traps to capture dragons.*

*Achmad uses a scale to weigh a juvenile dragon.*

The future for Komodo dragons looks good, because of laws that protect both them and their habitat.

These magnificent giants may rule their islands for centuries, thanks to the many people who care about them.

# Indonesia: Facts in Brief

**Number of islands:** 17,508, of which only about 6,000 are inhabited by people
**Most populated island:** Java
**Capital:** Jakarta, on the island of Java
**Official language:** Bahasa Indonesia
**Landscape:** about 60 active volcanoes

# Komodo Dragon Life Cycle

Male Komodo dragons fight with one another to win females. After mating, the females dig their nests and lay eggs inside. Females often lie on top of their nests and protect their eggs from predators. The eggs hatch after about eight months, just after the short rainy season ends, when insects are abundant. Small Komodo dragons are eaten by lots of predators—including larger Komodo dragons. These lizards can live for fifty years, though thirty years is more common. They keep growing a little each year until some reach 10 feet (3 meters).

# Smelling Their Environment

Komodo dragons detect food mainly by chemical cues, much the way snakes do. They swing their heads back and forth as they flick their forked tongues in and out of their mouths, sampling the air. When they stick their tongues back into their mouths, the two tongue tips transfer chemicals to special sacs called Jacobson's organs, located on the roof of the mouth. The system is so sensitive that if the concentration of molecules— for example, the smell of a deer— is stronger on the right tongue tip than on the left, the lizard senses that the deer is approaching from its right side. You do the same thing with your ears. If you hear a sound coming in louder on your right side, you know the sound is coming from that direction.

These lizards also pick up chemicals by touching their tongues to the ground. Again, the molecules are transferred from their tongue tips to the Jacobson's organs. Komodo dragons leave their grayish-white, smelly droppings out in the open. When a dragon comes upon a dropping, it stops to investigate. It tongue-flicks the pellet—sometimes for ten minutes— and presumably learns about the size and age of the dragon that deposited it and how recently the owner left it. By depositing their droppings in conspicuous areas, Komodo dragons might lay claim to hunting trails. The pellets might announce, "This area has been taken."

# Conservation Status

Komodo dragons are listed as "vulnerable" on the 2008 Red List of the International Union for the Conservation of Nature and Natural Resources (IUCN). This designation means that the species is likely to become endangered unless the circumstances threatening its survival and reproduction improve. There are only three thousand to five thousand Komodo dragons alive in the wild. Many scientists already consider them endangered.

Indonesian law protects the dragons. Without a permit, it is illegal to catch or kill these lizards or to disturb their nests.

The dragons are also protected under international law. They are listed on appendix 1 of the Convention on International Trade in Endangered Species (CITES). It is illegal to sell living or dead Komodo dragons or their skins taken from the wild.

# Komodo Survival Program

KOMODO SURVIVAL PROGRAM

The Komodo Survival Program (KSP) is a nonprofit organization that was established in 2007 to learn more about Komodo dragons. The ultimate goal of KSP is to protect and conserve the lizards. KSP is headquartered in Denpasar, Bali, Indonesia. Researchers are currently studying the lizards' population and feeding and nesting ecology. KSP's scientific advisers are three of the world's Komodo dragon experts: Dr. Tim Jessop, from Australia; Dr. Claudio Ciofi, from Italy; and Putra Sastrawan, from Indonesia. For more information on KSP, visit the organization's Web site: www.kspindonesia.org.

*A portion of the proceeds from this book will be donated to the Komodo Survival Program.*

# Bibliography

Auffenberg, K., and W. Auffenberg. Introduction: the past to now, pp. 1–19 in *Komodo Dragons: Biology and Conservation*, edited by Murphy, J. B., C. Ciofi, C. de La Panouse, and T. Walsh. Washington, DC: Smithsonian Institution Press, 2002.

Auffenberg, W. 1972. Komodo dragons. *Natural History* 81(4):52–59.

Auffenberg, W. *The Behavioral Ecology of the Komodo Monitor*. Gainesville, FL: University Presses of Florida, 1981.

Burden, D. 1927. The quest for the dragon of Komodo. *Natural History* 27(1):3–18.

Burden, W. D. 1927. Stalking the dragon lizard on the island of Komodo. *National Geographic* 52(2):216–33.

Burden, W. D. 1928. Results of the Douglas Burden expedition to the island of Komodo. V. Observations on the habits and distribution of *Varanus komodoensis* Ouwens. *American Museum Novitates* 316:1–10.

Ciofi, C. 1999. The Komodo dragon. *Scientific American* 280(3):84–91.

Ciofi, C. Conservation genetics, pp. 129–164 in *Komodo Dragons: Biology and Conservation*, edited by Murphy, J. B., C. Ciofi, C. de La Panouse, and T. Walsh. Washington, DC: Smithsonian Institution Press, 2002.

Ciofi, C., M. A. Beaumont, I. R. Swingland, and M. W. Bruford. 1999. Genetic divergence and units for conservation in the Komodo dragon *Varanus komodoensis*. *Proceedings of the Royal Society of London B* 266:2269–2274.

Ciofi, C., B. R. Smith, and M. Hutchins. Conservation: in situ and ex situ contributions, pp. 211–230 in *Komodo Dragons: Biology and Conservation*, edited by Murphy, J. B., C. Ciofi, C. de La Panouse, and T. Walsh. Washington, DC: Smithsonian Institution Press, 2002.

Dunn, E. R. 1927. Results of the Douglas Burden expedition to the island of Komodo. I. Notes on *Varanus komodoensis*. *American Museum Novitates* 286:1–10.

Gillespie, D., T. Fredeking, and J. M. Montgomery. Microbial biology and immunology, pp. 118–26 in *Komodo Dragons: Biology and Conservation*, edited by Murphy, J. B., C. Ciofi, C. de La Panouse, and T. Walsh. Washington, DC: Smithsonian Institution Press, 2002.

Jessop, T. S., J. Sumner, H. Rudiharto, D. Purwandana, M. J. Imansyah, J. A. Phillips. 2004. Distribution, use and selection of nest type by Komodo dragons. *Biological Conservation* 117:463–470.

Kern, J. A. 1968. Dragon lizards of Komodo. *National Geographic* December 1968:872–880.

King, D. R., E. R. Pianka, and B. Green. Biology, ecology, and evolution, pp. 23–41 in *Komodo Dragons: Biology and Conservation*, edited by Murphy, J. B., C. Ciofi, C. de La Panouse, and T. Walsh. Washington, DC: Smithsonian Institution Press, 2002.

Lutz, D., and J. M. Lutz. *Komodo: The Living Dragon*. 2nd ed. Salem, OR: Dimi Press, 1997.

Montgomery, J. M., D. Gillespie, P. Sastrawan, T. M. Fredeking, and G. L. Stewart. 2002. Aerobic salivary bacteria in wild and captive Komodo dragons. *Journal of Wildlife Diseases* 38:545–551.

Murphy, J. B., and T. Walsh. 2006. Dragons and humans. *Herpetological Review* 37(3):269–275.

Sastrawan, P., and C. Ciofi. Population distribution and home range, pp. 42–77 in *Komodo Dragons: Biology and Conservation*, edited by Murphy, J. B., C. Ciofi, C. de La Panouse, and T. Walsh. Washington, DC: Smithsonian Institution Press, 2002.

Shnayerson, M., and M. J. Plotkin. *The Killers Within: The Deadly Rise of Drug-Resistant Bacteria*. Boston: Little, Brown and Company, 2002.

Watts, P. C., K. R. Buley, S. Sanderson, W. Boardman, C. Ciofi, and R. Gibson. 2006. Parthenogenesis in Komodo dragons. *Nature* 444:1021–1022.

# Author's Note

I am most grateful to all the dragon admirers who have carried out fieldwork on Komodo dragons, cared for the lizards in captivity, and studied their reproduction and bacteria in the laboratory. I have consulted their published papers and communicated with many of them to write this book. The Fredeking quotes come from *The Killers Within*, written by Michael Shnayerson and Mark J. Plotkin. I thank the following people for permission to use their photographs: Achmad Ariefiandy, Kurt Auffenberg and family, Judith Bryja and the Houston Zoo, Jessie Cohen and the National Zoological Park, Jeri Imansyah, Charlie Mann and the Houston Zoo, and Jim Stout. Thanks also go to plateauAuthors, my writing buddies.

# Glossary

**antibiotic** medicine that fights infection-causing bacteria

**bacteria** tiny one-celled organisms that live almost everywhere

**biotechnology** use of living organisms to make medicines and other products

**cannibal** animal that eats live individuals of its same species

**chromosome** threadlike structure in a cell that carries genetic material

**forage** to search for food

**herpetologist** biologist who studies amphibians and reptiles

**mangrove forest** coastline forest made up of mangrove trees

**monitor** member of the lizard family Varanidae

**parthenogenesis** development of an individual from an unfertilized egg

**predator** animal that hunts other animals for food

**prey** animal that is hunted for food by a predator

**radio transmitter** device that transmits signals; when the device is attached to an animal, the researcher can receive these signals and track the animal

**savanna** area of grassland with scattered trees

# Further Reading

Darling, Kathy. *Komodo Dragon*. New York: Lothrop, Lee & Shepard, 1997.

Glaser, Jason. *Komodo Dragons*. Mankato, MN: Capstone Press, 2006.

Kalman, Bobbie. *Endangered Komodo Dragons*. New York: Crabtree Publishing, 2004.

Lunis, Natalie. *Komodo Dragon: The World's Biggest Lizard*. New York: Bearport Publishing, 2007.

Martin, James. *Komodo Dragons: Giant Lizards of Indonesia*. Mankato, MN: Capstone Press, 1995.

Myers, Jack. *On the Trail of the Komodo Dragon and Other Explorations of Science in Action*. Honesdale, PA: Boyds Mills Press, 1999.

Welsbacher, Anne. *Komodo Dragons*. Mankato, MN: Capstone Press, 2002.

## Web Sites*

National Geographic Kids
    kids.nationalgeographic.com/Animals/CreatureFeature/Komodo-dragon

Komodo Survival Program (KSP)
    www.kspindonesia.org

*Active at time of publication

# Index

antibiotics, 21
Ariefiandy, Achmad, 28–29
Auffenberg, Elinor, 10
Auffenberg, Kurt, 2, 10–11, 13
Auffenberg, Walter, 10, 12–16, 28

bacteria, 16–21, 27
blind, 6, 12, 13
Bryja, Judith, 26–27
Burden, W. Douglas, 6–8, 14

Ciofi, Claudio, 33

deer, 3, 6, 14, 15, 31
dragon, Komodo
 ambush hunting in, 14
 blood, 20–21
 burrows, 21, 28
 chromosomes, 22–23
 droppings, 14, 31
 eating behavior, 6–7, 10, 14–17, 18, 30
 eggs, 22–24, 25, 30
 fighting among, 18, 19, 30
 gums, 18
 hatchlings, 22–24
 lifespan, 30

marking (for identification), 12–13
nests, 22, 30, 32, 33
parthenogenesis, 23
personalities, 8, 12, 24–27
play behavior, 24–25
protection of, 9, 28–29, 32, 33
saliva, 16–21, 27
size, 2, 4, 7, 30
space needed, 12
swimming behavior, 8
teeth, 2, 6, 7, 18
tongues, 2, 4, 7, 20, 31
trapping, 7, 13, 29
tunnels, 11

Fredeking, Terry, 18–21

Hensbroek, van, 4

Indonesia, 2–4, 24, 28, 30, 32, 33
infection, 16–18, 21

Jacobson's organ, 31
Jessop, Tim, 33

King, F. Wayne, 10
Komodo dragon. See dragon, Komodo
Komodo Island, 2, 3, 4, 6, 11, 20–21, 29
Komodo National Park, 3, 28
Komodo Survival Program, 28, 33

Lesser Sunda Islands, 2–4

monitor lizard, 4
mythological dragon, 4, 5, 22

radio transmitter, 12
rat, black, 14
Reagan, President, 24

Sastrawan, Putra, 2, 11, 13, 28, 33
scale (for weighing), 29
Soeharto, President, 24

turtle, 6

water buffalo, 14
wild boar, 6, 7, 14, 16

zoos, 2, 8–9, 10, 22, 24, 26

# For Cyra and Kiyan —*M.C.*

A portion of the proceeds from this book will be donated to the Komodo Survival Program.

**Image Credits**
Covers (front and back) and pages 2 (left), 4, 6, 7, 10, 14, 15, 18, 19, 22: Achmad Ariefiandy; pages 1, 21, 28: Jim Stout; pages 2 (right), 11, 12, 13, 16, 20: courtesy of Kurt Auffenberg and family; page 3: John Nez; page 5, Eujin Kim Neilan, from the book *Imagine a Dragon* by Laurence Pringle, used by permission from Boyds Mills Press; pages 8, 17, 29: M. Jeri Imansyah; pages 9, 25, 26: Judith Bryja; pages 23, 24: Jessie Cohen; page 27: Charlie Mann.

Text copyright © 2010 by Marty Crump

Boyds Mills Press, Inc.
815 Church Street
Honesdale, Pennsylvania 18431
Printed in the United States of America

ISBN: 978-1-59078-757-1

Library of Congress Control Number: 2010925566

First edition
The text of this book is set in 13-point ITC Century.

10 9 8 7 6 5 4 3 2 1